辛亥革命

THE
CHINESE
REVOLUTION
OF 1911

by C. T. Liang

ASIA IN THE MODERN WORLD, NO. 1

THE CHINESE REVOLUTION OF 1911

Chin-Tung Liang

梁 敬 錞

St. John's University Press, Jamaica, New York
1962

Published under the auspices of the
Institute of Asian Studies, St. John's University

FOREWORD

Knowledge of the Far East is America's best weapon against the corroding influences of those who would distort the historical and cultural heritage of the Oriental peoples. Ignorance of the facts of history and the value of traditional Oriental cultures breeds apathy, indifference, and moral confusion when we are confronted with false propaganda. Wherever we are in doubt or error we are vulnerable to persuasion.

Under the able and dedicated direction of Dr. Paul K. T. Sih and his colleagues, the Institute of Asian Studies at St. John's University has proved—in the short span of three years—an effective instrument for the dissemination of knowledge through its treble program of graduate instruction, research, and publications, including admirable translations of the Oriental classics and scholarly interpretations of Oriental philosophy.

Distinguished scholars and specialists, in this series of monographs on "Asia in the Modern World," carefully describe and recreate the major events which have revolutionized Asia since 1900, presenting (often for the first time in English) firsthand accounts which are vital for understanding the nature of the struggles and the stakes involved. Proud of and confident in the efforts of the Institute of Asian Studies, we look to "The Chinese Revolution of 1911" by C. T. Liang to contribute substantially to the bulwark of truth.

EDWARD J. BURKE, C.M.
President
St. John's University

PREFACE

The Institute of Asian Studies at St. John's University, New York, in fulfilling the present need of the American academic world for Oriental Studies, publishes a series of monographs on *Asia in the Modern World.* Particular emphasis is placed on the political, social, economic, and cultural developments of China from the revolutionary period up to the present period of Communist domination.

Many Western scholars have written on modern China. Yet few have based their study on original source materials, much less on personal experience. The Institute is pleased to have several distinguished Chinese scholars as contributors. In most cases, they personally witnessed or participated in these historical events of contemporary China. Their accounts of these events contain most valuable source materials which cannot now be found elsewhere in the Western world.

In the present volume we find a special study on "The Chinese Revolution of 1911" by Mr. C. T. Liang. An eminent scholar and jurist, Mr. Liang is a recognized authority on the modern history of China. He taught history and literature for several years at the National

University of Peking. He is the author of several books, including *A History of the First World War* (Peking: Oriental Press, 1921) and *Extraterritoriality in China* (Shanghai: Commercial Press, 1931).

This study provides, for the first time in English, a detailed account of the events that led to the Chinese Revolution of 1911, together with new information on the Revolution itself and the turbulent years that followed it. The monograph is based upon exhaustive research in source materials, some of which are no longer available, and upon personal relations with those who actively participated in the events described. The author has also made use of unpublished private papers.

Proper names of persons, titles, places, organizations, movements, and so forth, are listed in English and Chinese at the end of this study.

Paul K. T. Sih, *Director*
Institute of Asian Studies
St. John's University

THE CHINESE REVOLUTION OF 1911

On October 10, 1911, Hsiung Ping-k'un, a soldier of the Engineering Battalion of the New Army stationed in Wu-ch'ang, shot and killed his commander, T'ao Ch'i-sheng. This was the first shot of the Revolution. The whole Battalion rose in revolt. In 48 days, it spread to fourteen provinces. In 81 days, the Chinese Republic was established and Dr. Sun Yat-sen was elected the provisional president. Forty-two days later, the Manchu Emperor issued an edict abdicating his throne, thus marking the end of two hundred and sixty-seven years of Manchu rule as well as the end of the system of monarchy in China. Following the Manchu abdication, Dr. Sun gave up the presidency in favor of Yuan Shih-k'ai, a position Dr. Sun had acquired after more than twenty years of revolutionary effort.

The end of Manchu rule

Although many books, both in the Chinese and Western languages, have dealt with this episode, I have always felt that its historical significance and artistic quality have yet to be properly evaluated. The German historian Karl R. Kopper said that the meaning of history must be determined by the future.[1] The English historian Arnold Toynbee thought that it would be better to use a telescope rather than a microscope in studying history.[2] The farther we are from a historical event the better we can see the underlying factors. If we are too close to the event, the historical data we have at our disposal would be incomplete.

Moreover, we would find it difficult to free ourselves from current bias and prejudice, and these would inevitably becloud the issues. Thus, in discussing this historical episode, which took place 50 years ago, we are looking at the event from a suitable distance. From this vantage point, I hope to be able to discern the principal features.

Two features of the Revolution

From the point of view of the history of world revolutions, there are at least two features of the 1911 Revolution which should be stressed. First, it was a double revolution. It was a revolt against alien rule as well as against despotic rule. Second, the upheaval took the form of a national revolution to bring about a social evolution. Most people are familiar with the first feature. To understand the second feature, it is necessary to have a knowledge of Eastern sociology and Confucian philosophy, for this was a revolution which embodied the unique revolutionary art of the East and the Confucian culture based on the Doctrine of the Mean. If we look back at Chinese history, we can see how this pattern of culture operated from the earliest times of the sage kings, who abdicated in favor of the worthy, and the revolutions of T'ang (founder of the Shang Dynasty) and Wu Wang (founder of the Chou Dynasty), down to the 1911 Revolution, when one-family rule was supplanted by a republican form of government. What we see in Chinese history is very different from the Cromwellian Revolution in England, the French Revolution and the Russian Revolution. Perhaps, it was precisely because of the operation of the Doctrine of the Mean that the revolution was not a thorough one. Indeed, it sowed many seeds of trouble for the future. However, as Tolstoy said, history is "a tissue of disconnected accidents." In discussing the events, we must point out the special features of the disconnected accidents so as to arrive at the true meaning of this historical episode.

Sowing the Seeds

The seeds of the 1911 Revolution were sown mainly by Dr. Sun Yat-sen. Dr. Sun's idea of racial revolution took shape a year after the Sino-French War of 1884-85, while his idea of political revolution was formed a year after the Sino-Japanese War of 1894-95. These revolutionary ideas were first put into practice mainly after the Russo-Japanese War of 1904-05. The foreign aggression from which China suffered in the second half of the nineteenth century was thus the precursor of the 1911 Revolution, and the new international situation in the Far East in the twentieth century was its stimulant.

Sun's revolutionary effort

In the sixteen years between 1895 and 1911, Dr. Sun made a total of ten revolutionary attempts. (See Table A.) He took part personally in only two of them. In 1895 he was expelled by the Hong Kong Government; in 1906 by the Japanese Government; and in 1907 by the Annamese Government. Unable to establish himself in Hong Kong, Japan, and other areas in Southeast Asia, he was obliged to entrust the task of front-line revolutionary activities to Huang K'e-ch'iang and Hu Han-min, leaving to himself the task of organizing the party and raising funds.

Table A
Revolutionary Uprisings Before 1911

Date, Place	Persons in Charge	Groups Involved	Circumstances	Additional Notes
Oct. 26, 1895 Canton	Sun Yat-sen, Lu Hao-tung, Cheng Kuei-kuang	Salt Administration Police and army veterans	Failed owing to exposure of plot. Lu Hao-tung killed	
Oct. 1, 1900 San Chou T'ien in Hui-chou	Cheng Shih-liang, Shih Chien-ju	The Triad Society, the Salt Administration Police	Failed owing to lack of support	Shih Chien-ju & Yamada Yoshimasa killed
Aug. 9, 1906 Ch'i Nu Hu in Hui-chou	Teng Tzu-yu	The Triad Society	The uprising lasted 4 days	
May 22, 1907 Huang Kang in Ch-'ao-chou	Sun Yat-sen, Hsu Hsueh-ch'iu	Hung Men Hui	One day uprising. Kayano Yoshitomo.	
Sept. 4, 1907 Fang Ch'eng	Huang K'e-ch'iang, Wang Ho-shun	Arrangement with the New Army for support failed	2 month uprising failed owing to lack of support	Withdrew to Shih Wang Ta Shan
Dec. 1, 1907 Chen-nan-kuan	Huang K'e-ch'iang, Hu Han-min, & Ike Kyokichi	Arrangement with Defense Patrol Battalion for support failed	Occupied Chen-nan-kuan for 7 days. Failed owing to ammunition shortage	Withdrew to Annam
Sept. 4, 1907 Shan-ssu in Ch'ing-lien	Huang-K'e-ch'iang, Huang Ming-t'ang	Arrangement with New Army for support	Failed owing to lack of supplies	Withdrew
Apr. 29, 1908 Ho-k'ou in Yunnan	Hu Han-min, Huang Ming-t'ang	Arrangement with Defense Patrol Battalion for support	Captured Ho-k'ou and Meng-tzu. Failed after resisting for several months	France declared neutrality
Feb. 10, 1910 Heng-chi-kang (Canton)	Ni Ying-tien	New Army mutinied	Failed owing to lack of supplies	Ni Ying-tien killed
Apr. 27, 1911 Huang-hua-Kang (Canton)	Huang K'e-ch'iang, Chao Sheng	Support of the New Army	Failed owing to faulty coordination	Death of the 72 martyrs

In these ten attempts two points are worth our attention. First, the places chosen for the revolution were mostly in the coastal area. Second, the revolutionary activities took place mostly after the Russo-Japanese War. The first point involved the dispute over revolutionary strategy between the Liang-Hu (Hunan and Hupeh) clique, led by Sung Chiao-jen, and the Liang-Kwang (Kwangtung and Kwangsi) clique, led by Chu Chih-hsing. The second point is a reflection of the growth of anti-Manchu forces after the formation of the T'ung Meng Hui in 1905. In general, we may say that the secret societies were mostly responsible for the revolutionary attempts before 1906, while the students were mostly responsible for the attempts between 1906 and 1908. After 1908, the New Army was almost wholly responsible.

In these twenty years of revolutionary activity, the period of seed-sowing lasted ten years, the period of fertilizing lasted nine years, while the period of fruition took only 48 days. We can still remember how in 1911 Manchu Banner troops could be frightened into submission by a show of white wrist bands (revolutionary emblems), and how rumors appearing in newspapers could cause the fall of towns and cities to the revolutionaries. It was all like child's play but we should not forget that the ease with which the revolution was achieved was a clear demonstration of the effectiveness of the work of the revolutionary fathers.

During the period of seed-sowing, the revolutionary organization consisted of the Hsing

Three periods of revolutionary activity

Chung Hui, organized in 1895, and the T'ung Meng Hui, organized in 1905. The difference between the Hsing Chung Hui and the T'ung Meng Hui may be seen from the wordings of their initiation oaths. The Hsing Chung Hui oath contained the following words: "Revive China and maintain the national entity." It was very vague about democracy and the people's livelihood. The oath of the T'ung Meng Hui contained the following stirring words: "Expel the Tartars, revive China, establish a republic and equalize the land."[3] The latter oath was an expression of Sun Yat-sen's ideas of the Three People's Principles. It also symbolized the beginning of the idea of the Chinese Republic. This idea was formed in Brussels, Berlin, Paris, and Tokyo in the same year (1905). It was not until this time that Dr. Sun began to feel that students were qualified to take part in the revolution and that the revolution could be achieved during his lifetime.[4]

Six independent uprisings

In addition to the ten revolutionary attempts, there were six independent uprisings. (See Table B.) This shows that Dr. Sun Yat-sen was not the only person who laid the groundwork for the 1911 Revolution. The Revolution was the result of various forces.

T'ang Ts'ai-ch'ang and Lin Kuei, mentioned in Table B, were disciples of K'ang Yu-wei and Liang Ch'i-ch'ao. Hung Ch'uan-fu took part in the T'ai-p'ing Rebellion. Yu Chih-mo and Liu Tao-i were fighters of the Hua Hsing Society, while Hsu Hsi-ling, Ch'iu Ching, and Hsiung Ch'eng-chi belonged to the Kuang Fu Society.[5] Most of these men — Hsu Hsi-ling,

Table B
Six Independent Revolutionary Attempts Before 1911

Date, Place	Persons in Charge	Groups Involved	Circumstances	Notes
Aug.-Sept. 1900 Hankow & Ta-t'ung in Anhwei	T'ang Ts'ai-ch'ang, Lin Kuei, Shen Chin	Fu Yu Piao, Kao Lao Hui, Tzu Li Hui	Plot exposed. Both T'ang & Lin killed	Dated calendar from the Yellow Emperor era
Aug. 1902 Canton	Hung Chuan-fu, Li Chi-t'ang	Hung Meng Hui in Canton & Hongkong	Plot exposed. Liang Mu-hsing killed	Used "Ta Ming Shun T'ien Kuo" as title
Oct. 1904 Changsha	Huang Hsing, Ma Fu-i, Liu K'uei-i	Kao Lao Hui	Plot uncovered before uprising	Chang Chi accompanied Huang Hsing
Nov. 1906 P'ing-hsiang, Li-ling, and Liu-yang	Yu Chih-mo, Liu Tao-i	Workers, soldiers & Kao Lao Hui	Uprising held out for a few months	Yu, Liu killed
June, 1907 Anking	Hsu Hsi-ling, Ch'iu Ching	Kuang Fu Hui	Attempt to assassinate Eng Ming failed	Used title "Kung Ho" for dating
Nov. 22, 1908 Anking	Hsiung Ch'eng-chi	Artillery Battalion of the New Army	Uprising collapsed in 1 day	Hsiung also a member of Kuang Fu Hui

for example — did not recognize Dr. Sun's leadership. Some even bitterly opposed Dr. Sun (such as T'ao Ch'eng-chang of the Kuang Fu Society).[6] In raising the standard of revolt, some dated their calendar from the reign of the legendary Yellow Emperor, some from the Ming Dynasty, and some used the title Kung Ho. Although they all failed, they did their part in sowing the seeds of the revolution.

Watering and Fertilizing

The political failure of the Manchu Court before 1900 was different from the political failure after 1900. Before 1900, the political failure was caused by the struggle for power between the Emperor, Kuang-hsü, on the one hand, and the Empress Dowager and the stubbornness and arrogance of the Court on the other. After 1900, the political failure was due to nepotism on the part of the Manchu aristocrats and universal corruption. The Empress Dowager Tz'u-hsi of the post-Boxer era might have been more enlightened than the Emperor of 1898, but Empress Lung Yü (Emperor Kuang-hsü's widow) after 1908 was more corrupt than Tz'u-hsi before 1900.

Empress Dowager's reform measures

Upon her return from Sian, Empress Dowager Tz'u-hsi undertook reform measures on a large scale.[7] In 1902, the Imperial Civil Service Examination was abolished and schools were established. (Government financial aid for elementary schools and promotion of elementary and middle-school education and normal education were implemented.) In 1903, a police system was begun and the bureaucratic system was changed. In 1904, a new army was formed and studies of the constitutional government were begun. In 1906, it was decreed that the smoking of opium would be prohibited within ten years and a constitutional system would be established within nine years. In 1907, preparations were made for local self-government. In social reform, the Empress Dowager also showed progressive tendencies. For instance, Chinese-Manchu inter-marriage was encouraged, women's foot-binding prohibited, contributions of private funds were made to promote the education of women, and the eunuch system came very close to being abolished. All these reforms were discussed in detail in Meribeth E. Cameron's doctoral thesis: "The Reform Movement in China—1898-1912." For this reason, in recent years some Westerners studying the Chinese history of this period attributed a good part of China's modernization to Tz'u-hsi, thinking that it was she who laid the foundation. They also believed that while Westernization had strengthened Japan, it brought about the downfall of the Manchu Dynasty.[8] This is, of course, a superficial view.

In fact, it is quite fair to say that the Manchu Court fully deserved the fate that befell it in 1911. Besides the prevalence of nepotism and corruption, the Manchu Court was plagued by two other factors: it attempted the centralization of political power without possessing political capacity, and it carried out political oppression without having actual power. For instance, the object of establishing a new bureaucratic system was to reduce the discrimination by the Manchus against the Chinese. However, of the twelve new ministries under the new cabinet, eight important ministries were headed by Manchus, while the remaining cabinet posts, which were of little importance, were left to the Chinese.[9] Of the eight ministries headed by Manchus, five were given to members of the royal family. The Prince Regent, Tsai-feng, was Jung Lu's son-in-law. The Minister of Finance, Tsai Tse, was Em-

Corruption of the Manchu Court

press Lung Yü's brother-in-law. Tsai Hsün headed the Ministry of Navy and Tsai T'ao was the Chief of Staff. Both were Tsai Feng's brothers. Ying Ch'ang and Shan Ch'i headed the Army and the police force respectively.[10]

As for corruption, the situation was even worse. Official positions of the Court were for sale at stipulated prices. Even the adoption of such political measures as the granting of amnesty to members of the K'ang-Liang Party required bribery.[11] I K'uang, the Prime Minister, and Sheng Hsuan-huai, the Minister of Communications, were well known for their greed. Sheng obtained his post by bribing I K'uang. I K'uang's son was involved in a scandal with an actress.[12]

Collapse imminent

With political corruption reaching a new low, a collapse was only to be expected. Ever since the T'ai-p'ing Rebellion (1850-1864), the Manchu Government had been depending upon the viceroys of the great provinces to put down internal unrest. After the Hsien-feng and T'ung-chih emperors, power shifted from the central government to the provinces. While decentralization was not in itself a sound system, the results became much more serious when the central government was without both power and capacity. In all fairness, Sheng Hsuan-huai's policy of nationalizing the main railway lines was sound. However, behind the nationalization policy were the loans of the Four Power Consortium, and behind the loans was the wrangle among the royal relatives for their share of the commission. Moreover, the measures proposed for dealing with the private shares of the Szechwan-Hankow and Canton-Hankow railroads were vague and unfair. Finally, strong-arm measures, involving arrests and killings, were used in dealing with the railroad petitioners.[13] This brought about a general strike in Chengtu and the declaration of independence at Jung-hsien. (The declaration of independence at Jung-hsien ante-dated that of Wu-ch'ang by 25 days.) The whole country was about to erupt like a volcano. The eruption came at Wu-ch'ang.

Also, newspaper propaganda constituted an effective fertilizer that nourished the 1911 Revolution. The most important Chinese papers at that time were the *Hsin-min Ts'ung-pao* and the *Min Pao* in Tokyo. The former was the party organ of K'ang Yu-wei and Liang Ch'i-ch'ao and the latter the organ of the T'ung Meng Hui. The most violently anti-Manchu paper in the country was the Shanghai *Su Pao* with Chang Shih-ch'ao as the editor-in-chief. Several writers were arrested at this time for their writings. Chang T'ai-yen was imprisoned together with Tsou Jung in the police station in Shanghai.[14] The latter was a Szechwanese. His book, *The Revolutionary Army,* and Chen Tien-hua's two books, *Ching Shih Chung* ("A Bell to Alert the World") and *Meng Hui T'ou* ("Turn Around Fast"), were among the most influential revolutionary works of the period between 1903 and 1905. Tsou Jung died in prison. The oppressive measures of the Manchu Government against the Chinese students in Japan prompted Chen T'ien-hua to commit suicide. These works thus

Oppression of revolutionary writings

became all the more popular. Chen's *Ching Shih Chung* and *Meng Hui T'ou* contained songs written to the rhythm of popular tunes. The songs were full of nationalistic and revolutionary sentiments. I knew quite a few stanzas during my youth. Even now I can remember a few lines:

> *All we want is to recover our land and they say that is rebellion! It is the shameless ones who would fight for them!*
> *We are only afraid of being like India, unable to defend our land; we are only afraid of being like Annam, of having no hope of reviving. We are only afraid of being like Poland, the Poles who drift about in an alien land; we are only afraid of being like the Jews, the Jews who are without a home!*

Continuing, they sang:

> *We Chinese have no part in this China of ours. This dynasty exists only in name! Being slaves of the foreigners, they force us common people to call them masters!*

Effective propaganda

These two propaganda works went through many editions. Millions of copies were printed and circulated among the schools, the barracks, and the countryside. The Manchu Government was unable to impose an effective ban on them. Racial consciousness infected the youth of the whole country. That the Chinese soldiers and police refused to fight for the Manchus during the 1911 Revolution was due in part to these popular songs.

We shall now discuss the role of the intellectuals. Among the intellectuals, the Japanese-returned students and members of the Tzu I Chu, or provincial assemblies, were the more important elements. The number of Chinese students in Japan rose sharply following the establishment by Fan Yuan-lien of a short-course school. In 1904, there were only six hundred Chinese students in Japan. By 1905, the number had increased to two thousand and four hundred; by 1906, to eight thousand and six hundred; by 1907, to ten thousand; and by 1911, to more than twenty thousand.[15] The interest the students showed in national affairs at this time was certainly as high as during the period of the May Fourth Movement. While the May Fourth Movement was directed against Japan, Russia was at this time the opponent. The Russians remained in occupation of Manchuria from 1900 to the Russo-Japanese War. This infuriated the Chinese students in Japan. They organized a volunteer group and appealed to the government through elected delegates to let them fight the Russians. (Mr. Niu Yung-chien, who is now in New York, was one of the delegates.)

Students' interest in national affairs

Instead of diverting this patriotic spirit into the proper channel and putting it to good use, the Manchu Government sought to suppress it. As a result, the students of Nanyang College went on strike, patriotic societies were organized, and the movement spread to Nanking. Having failed in their request to fight the Russians, the Tokyo students began to organize themselves through their provincial societies and returned to China to take part in revolutionary activities. The most influential groups among them at this time were the Hunan, Hupeh, and Chekiang groups. The Hunan group organized the Hua Hsing Hui under Huang K'e-ch'iang and Liu K'uei-i. The Hupeh group organized the Kung Chin Hui under Chü Cheng and Sun Wu. The Chekiang group organized the Kuang Fu Hui under Ts'ai Yuan-p'ei, Chang T'ai-yen, and T'ao Ch'eng-chang. The Hua Hsing Hui maintained contact with the secret societies in the upper Yangtze area. The Kung Chin Hui sought to bring about the disaffection of the New Army and the defense patrols. The Kuang Fu Hui resorted to the assassination of Manchus. Each of these societies had achievements to its credit. (Readers may be surprised to find Mr. Ts'ai Yuan-p'ei, known to all of us as a great scholar and educator, serving as the leader of an assassination society at this time!)

The provincial assemblies

Provincial assemblies came into being in 1906 as a preparation for constitutionalism. They were called one year before the meeting of the Tzu-cheng Yuan (National Assembly). A candidate seeking election to the provincial assembly was required to be of the male sex, a middle-school graduate (or having equivalent educational background such as having passed the civil service examinations), and twenty-five years of age.[16] The election at that time seemed to be quite fair. Most of the representatives elected were enthusiastic and had a sense of responsibility. This was especially true of the presidents of the assemblies. They were mostly people who were popular in their localities. Most of the representatives to the assemblies advocated constitutional monarchy. They were backed by the Constitutional Society. They had the Kuo-min Kung-pao as their organ and such able men as T'ang Hua-lung, P'u Tien-chun, Lin Chang-min, and T'ang Shou-ch'ien as supporters. Liang Ch'i-ch'ao, who was then in Japan, served as the leader behind the scene.

The Manchu Government could very well make use of these representative institutions as buffers to ward off the revolution. It did not do so. Instead, it rejected their joint request for the immediate opening of parliament and resorted to high-handed measures. Although the Government finally shortened the period stipulated for constitutional preparation from nine years to five years, it treated the petitioners very harshly. Some were exiled to Sinkiang. The provincial assemblies thus became more radical and began to sympathize with the revolutionists. From the fact that most of the presidents of the assemblies became governors after the 1911 Revolution, we can see how influential they were at this time.

The Government rejects assemblies' requests

In 1910, the Constitutional Society petitioned the Government to (1) lift the ban on parties, (2) support constitutionalism, and (3) convene the parliament as soon as possible. The Government rejected all these requests. However, when the situation became more critical in 1911, it conceded on all these points. That, of course, did not stop the revolution. As Theodore Roosevelt once said, "The essence of wisdom is to be wise in time." The Manchu became wise too late!

The most important force that contributed

to the Revolution at this time was the New Army. Yuan Shih-k'ai began to train the New Army in 1904. According to the approved program, a total of thirty-six divisions were to be trained in the whole country. Each division was to have 12,512 officers and men.[17] The training of the Army was to be completed within seven years (by 1912). There were to be six divisions in North China, three in Hunan and Hupeh, and three in Kwangtung and Kwangsi. The other provinces were to have one or two divisions each. The training of the New Army was not carried out very energetically in the provinces. Consequently, by 1911 only fourteen divisions and twenty brigades were formed in the whole country. Among them, six divisions were in North China, one division and two brigades in Hupeh, and one division and one brigade in South China.

The training of the New Army

The New Army in North China differed from that in Hupeh and other provinces in South China in that the officers in the former were all from the Pao-ting Cadets Training School and the Chiang-wu Tang (Military Academy). No Japanese-trained cadets were used. It was thus less susceptible to the influence of revolutionary ideas. After the dismissal of Yuan Shih-k'ai early in 1907, the New Army in North China was at one time placed under the command of the members of the royal family. It was at this time that the Japanese-returned cadets, Chang Shao-tseng, Wu Lu-cheng, and Lan T'ien-wei, joined the Army.[18] This led to the episode at Luan-chou when the Army demanded reform by the Government, threatening to use military pressure. (When Dr. Sun Yat-sen told the American military strategist, Homer Lea, that he had control over several divisions in North China, he was referring to this.) [19]

The Manchus were not unaware of the fact that most of the officers and men of the New Army were anti-Manchu. (The Minister of War mentioned this to the American military attaché in 1908 and 1910.) [20] Nevertheless, they were obliged to recruit Chinese if they were to have a New Army at all. Moreover, as the Army increased in size, they found it necessary to use Japanese-trained cadets. The British military attaché in Peking made the remark that the Manchu Government was spending a large sum of money every year to train an anti-Manchu army.[21] From this we can see the dilemma of the time.

The Anti-Manchu attitude of the New Army

Besides the New Army, there were the defense patrol units, naval units, etc., in the provinces. These units were organized under the old military formation. Their uniforms, rations, and weapons were different from those of the New Army. Their viewpoints were also different. Taking advantage of this, the high officials would at times use the defense patrol units to keep an eye on the New Army. Sometimes, the arms of the New Army would be taken and given to these units. This, of course, created ill feeling in the New Army and abetted their revolutionary tendencies. This was the background of the military disintegration at this time.

Blossoming

The Revolution as described above may seem to have progressed from one stage to another in an orderly fashion. In point of fact, the Wu-ch'ang uprising was not planned. According to the available historical data, Sun Yat-sen and Huang K'e-ch'iang had planned for an uprising to take place in Canton in 1910. Owing to the collapse of Ni Ying-tien's attempt, the timing was changed, and the next attempt was to take place in 1911. The famous Huang-hua Kang uprising of April 27, 1911 took more than six months of intensive preparation. The Party concentrated its best talents for the effort and spent hundreds of thousands of dollars accumulated through contributions. Other provinces were expected to follow suit but the great attempt failed.[22] As it turned out, all the planned uprisings failed. The one that finally brought on the Revolution was least expected to succeed.

The Wu-ch'ang uprising was proposed by the Liang-Hu faction. After the Huang-hua Kang failure, Chü Cheng and T'an Jen-feng consulted Huang K'e-ch'iang and planned to stage an uprising at Yung P'ing during the Autumn military review during October-November.[23] However, on October 9 a bomb exploded accidentally in the revolutionary headquarters at Yu Ch'ing Li in Hankow. Some partisans were arrested and, most important of all, a list of the names of the party members was found. The authorities were now prepared to make arrests. As members of the New Army were involved, they were forced to act. They made

The Wu-ch'ang uprising not planned

18

Chiang I-wu of the Literary Society their commander-in-chief and planned to strike that very evening. However, owing to faulty signals that night, the raid on the headquarters, the arrests of Liu Yao-ch'eng and P'an Ch'u F'an, and Ch'iang I-wu's injury, the uprising was postponed till the following day. All this shows how tentative the whole undertaking was.

As to the military force that the revolutionaries were able to muster, there were only the troops of the engineering battalion, the army service corps and the artillery outside the city, totalling not more than three thousand men. On the other hand, the government troops outside the city numbered over ten thousand.[24]

Although the Wu-ch'ang uprising had taken place in such haste, the revolutionaries maintained a high degree of military discipline and conducted their diplomacy well. This was the principal reason for the speed with which the consular body recognized their status as insurgents. This was very important during the early stage of the revolution. From the Palace archives and the confidential diplomatic reports of foreign governments, we have now the following information concerning the first days of the revolution:

*Diplomacy helps
the Revolution*

On the second day of the outbreak, the Inspector of the Hankow Customs, Ch'i Yao-san, was ordered by Viceroy Jui Ch'eng to request the foreign consular body in Hankow to send boats to prevent the revolutionaries from crossing the river. On the fifth day of the outbreak, the Manchu Government asked Japan to send troops to put down the rebellion.[25] Sir

John Jordan, the British Minister, instructed the British consuls to have no dealings with the revolutionary army so as to avoid any misunderstanding on the part of the Manchu Government.[26] However, as soon as the consular body in Hankow received Hu Ying's assurance to respect foreign treaty rights,[27] they issued a joint declaration in Chinese on October 14 to maintain neutrality. This gave the revolutionary army an international status, and it had an important effect on the attitude of the other provinces.

Neutrality maintained by Foreign Powers

Table C on the following page shows the dates and the circumstances of the revolutionary uprisings in the various provinces. An analysis of the uprisings in various provinces brings out a number of points that are worth our attention.

First, with the exception of the revolts in Nanking, Sian, Foochow, and Yunnan, where some fighting took place, all the other provinces declared their independence peacefully. This shows to what extent the Wu-ch'ang revolution was a manifestation of the will of the people. Secondly, the response began mostly in November. There was little activity in the latter half of October. This shows that the various provinces were watching how the situation was going to develop before taking sides. Thirdly, after declaring independence, the new governments that were set up in the provinces had different titles and used different systems of dating. This shows that the 1911 Revolution did not have a unified command. Fourthly, the Five Color Flag was used in the various prov-

Table C

Uprisings in the Provinces Following the Wu-ch'ang Outbreak in 1911

Provinces	Dates	Titles Used	Personalities	Circumstances
Jung-hsien, Szechwan	Sept. 15	T'ung-chih Chun	Wang T'ien-chieh	Party as the nucleus with the New Army sympathetic
Chih-chiang, Szechwan	Nov. 21	Shu-pei Tu-tu	Tseng Sheng-chai	Party as the nucleus with the support of military trainees and students
Chungking, Szechwan	Nov. 22	Shu-chun Cheng-fu	Chang P'ei-chueh & Hsia Chih-shih (Deputy)	Party as the nucleus with participation of infantry and supply troops of the New Army
Chengtu, Szechwan	Nov. 27	Ta-han Chun-cheng-fu, Ssu-ch'uang Tu-tu	P'u Tien-chun & Chu Ching-lan	Elected by the Provincial Assembly and supported by the New Army
Sian, Shensi	Oct. 22	Fu-han-chun Ta-t'ung-ling	Chang Feng-hui & Ch'ien Ting (Deputy)	New Army as nucleus. Some fighting in Tartar City
Changsha, Hunan	Oct. 22	Chün-cheng-fu Tu-tu	Chiao Ta-feng (first) & T'an Yen-k'ai (later)	The Party, New Army and Provincial Assembly
Taiyuan, Shansi	Oct. 29	Chün-cheng-fu Tu-tu	Yen Hsi-shan & Wen Ching-an (Deputy)	New Army and Provincial Assembly took part
Kunming, Yunnan	Oct. 30	Chün-cheng-fu Tu-tu	Ts'ai O, Lo P'ei-chin, T'ang Chi-yao	Chiang-wu-t'ang (Military Academy) of the New Army took the initiative
Kiukiang, Kiangsi	Oct. 23	Chün-cheng-fu Tu-tu	Ma Yü-pao	Uprising of the New Army
Nanchang, Kiangsi	Nov. 2	Chün-cheng-fu Tu-tu	Wu Chieh-chang	Resolution of the Provincial Asembly and various circles
Kweiyang, Kweichow	Nov. 5	Lin-shih Cheng-fu	Yang Chin-ch'eng and Chao Ch'un-ch'eng (Deputy)	Party members took the initiative. Resolution of various circles

Provinces	Dates	Titles Used	Personalities	Circumstances
Shanghai Kiangsu	Nov. 5	Hu Chün-cheng-fu Tu-tu	Chen Ch'i-mei & Li P'ing-shu	Uprising started by the police and merchant organizations
Soochow, Kiangsu	Nov. 5	Chung-hua Min-kuo Chün-cheng-fu Kiang-su Tu-tu-fu	Ch'eng Te-ch'uan	Cooperation between party members and the New Army
Chinkiang, Kiangsu	Nov. 6	Chen-kiang Tu-tu	Lin Shu-ch'ing	Kuang-fu Hui as the nucleus with the cooperation of the New Army
Nanking, Kiangsu	Dec. 2	Lin-shih Cheng-fu	Hsu Shao-cheng and allied forces of Kiang-su and Chekiang	The New Army took the initiative. Fierce battle with Chang Hsun
Hangchow Chekiang	Nov. 6	Chün-cheng-fu Tu-tu	T'ang Shou-ch'lien	New Army took the initiative. The provincial Assembly was sympathetic
Ningpo, Chekiang	Nov. 6	Chün-cheng-fen-fu Tu-tu	Liu Hsun & Ch'ang Jung-ch'ing (Deputy)	Chosen by various circles in Ningpo
Shou-chou, Anhwei	Nov. 5	Tsung-ssu-ling	Wang Ch'ing-yün	Uprising started by Party members
Anking, Anhwei	Nov. 8	Tu-tu	Chu Chia-pao	Resolution of Provincial Assembly
Kweilin, Kiangsi	Nov. 6	Tu-tu	Lu Jung-t'ing	Resolution of Provincial Assembly
Canton, Kwangtung	Nov. 9	Tu-tu	Hu Han-min	Resolution of Provincial Assembly and the Army
Foochow, Fukien	Nov. 11	Ta-tu-tu	Sun Tao-jen	Resolution of Provincial Assembly. Minor battle with Manchu troops
Chefoo, Shantung	Dec. 12	Tai-li Tu-tu	Tu Ch'ien	An earlier declaration of independence in Shantung was withdrawn. The entry of the navy into Chefoo ordered by T'ung Meng Hui

inces. The Wu-ch'ang revolutionaries at first used a flag with two circles of nine stars each. The first flag symbolized the unity of the five races, while the second symbolized the eighteen provinces. Dr. Sun Yat-sen's design with a white star in a blue sky was never used, showing that Dr. Sun's faction did not have unified control. The provincial assemblies which advocated constitutional monarchy were, however, able to cooperate with the revolutionary party to bring about the revolution. This was truly a union of all the anti-Manchu forces in the country.

Besides the occupation of Nanking by Hsu Shao-cheng, the most important factors which contributed to the success of the 1911 Revolution were: (1) sympathy towards the revolution on the part of the middle and lower naval officers and men; and (2) demand for reform by Chang Shao-tseng, commander of the Twentieth Division at Luan-chou, backed and supported by military force.

Factors leading to success

When the revolution broke out at Wu-ch'ang, the Manchu Government dispatched Yin Ch'ang, the Minister of War, to take command of the armies of Feng Kuo-chang and Tuan Ch'i-jui against the Southern revolutionaries and ordered Sah Chen-ping, Vice-Minister of Navy, to proceed to Hankow with the cruisers Hai Yung, Hai Ch'ou, Hai Shen and a number of torpedo boats to support the action. Naval fire power was, of course, superior to anything that the revolutionaries had. Li Yuan-hung, the revolutionary commander, who was at one time a naval officer, was quite aware of this. However, at the battle of Ch'ing Shan in late October, the gunners on the cruisers were in contact with the revolutionaries. They purposely directed their gunfire away from their concentrations. This enabled the revolutionaries to hold their line and keep the city of Wu-ch'ang.[28]

The effects of the Luan-chou incident

The Luan-chou incident involving the demand of the military leaders occurred on October 27. That was on the eve of Feng Kuo-chang's occupation of Hankow. As the Twentieth Division belonged to the Pei-yang Army, and as it was in charge of army supplies, the action not only produced great nervousness in the Manchu Court but also among the Northern troops at the front. This episode was followed by Wu Lu-cheng's assassination and the transfer of Chang Shao-tseng. With the latter's transfer, Lan T'ien-wei was unable to act by himself. The threat thus died down in less than ten days. However, by this time the Manchu government had proclaimed the Constitutional Articles, dismissed the cabinet composed of members of the royal family, and changed its policy towards the revolutionaries. This strengthened the position of the revolutionary army, produced a band-wagon atmosphere in the provinces, and brought about a different outlook on the part of the diplomatic corps. Feng Kuo-chang's army halted in Hankow for ten days. This gave the revolutionaries a much needed respite to reorganize their forces. The Luan-chou affair thus contributed a great deal to the success of the 1911 Revolution. However, this action on the part of the army officers, which amounted almost to an ultimatum, became a precedent for the later warlords under the Republic. Later, when Tuan Ch'i-jui made his demands, he was following Chang Shao-tseng's example.

At this point, readers would naturally want to know what Dr. Sun Yat-sen was doing all this time and whether he had a part in the 1911 Revolution. Dr. Sun left the following account:

Sun's analysis of the situation

"I was in Denver, Colorado, the day after the revolution broke out in Wu-ch'ang. Ten days or so before the outbreak, I received a telegram from Huang Ke'-ch'iang asking for financial support for the action that was about to take place at Wu-ch'ang. As my secret code was being shipped by train, I was not able to decode the telegram. I did not reply to Huang, as it was late and I was tired. The next morning, news of the occupation of Wu-ch'ang by the Revolutionary Army appeared in the newspapers. I could return to China from the United States in a comparatively short time. However, on second thought, I changed my plan and decided to go to England and return by the Suez route, for I believed that I could be of help in the diplomatic arena. The diplomatic situation at the time was as follows: both the American Government and the American people were sympathetic towards our revolution. The British people were sympathetic but the British Government's attitude depended upon Japan. The German and Russian Governments were sympathetic to the Manchu Government, while the attitude of the Japanese Government was unpredictable. . . . Therefore, I thought of going to England to persuade the British to use their influence with the Japanese. At the same time, I wanted to ask the Four Power Banking Consortium there to stop the payment of loans to the Manchu Government. I managed to secure the agreement of the British Government on both points. I also wired Governor Chang Ming-ch'i to surrender the city of Canton in exchange for his life. This telegram was also effective."[29]

The diplomatic archives of the various governments that we now have at our disposal show how accurately Dr. Sun had analyzed the diplomatic situation of the time.[30] Although at the beginning of the revolution the Japanese Government had offered to put down the uprising for the Manchu Government through military intervention, the latter did not accede to its demands. After the Manchu Court had appointed Yuan Shih-k'ai, the Japanese wanted to intervene militarily on three occasions: the first time on October 15, 1911 (five days after the outbreak), the second time on December 7, and the third time on December 18. On the first occasion, the Japanese Government stated that if the rebellion should spread to Manchuria, the Japanese would send troops regardless of the attitude of the powers.[31] On the

Japan's three attempts at intervention

second occasion, Kokura's three divisions were ordered to prepare to leave Moji within 24 hours for Dairen and Peking (see Chinese Minister to Japan Wang Ta-hsieh's telegram to the Yuan cabinet, and American Military Attaché Shipley's telegram to the War Department). At this point, the German Government consulted the U.S. Government confidentially, the American Government inquired of the British Government about the matter, and the latter intervened with the Japanese three times. (The first protest the British lodged was when the Japanese Minister to China made a statement promising Yuan Shih-k'ai would support the Manchu Court. The second protest was against the extension of loans by the Japanese Government to the Manchu Government. The third protest was against the proposed Japanese military intervention.) If it had not been for the British action, Japan would have intervened.[32] That the British Government had taken such vigorous action was not unrelated to Dr. Sun's activities in London.

The forestalling of loans to the Manchu Government was also a serious blow to the Government. According to Sir John Jordan's report to the Foreign Office,[33] Empress Lung Yü sent thirty-three cases of gold bars (three million taels), handed down from Empress Dowager Ts'u-hsi, to the Hong Kong-Shanghai Banking Corporation in exchange for cash that was to be issued to the army. The seals on the cases and the markings on the gold bars showed that the bars had been accumulated for a period of more than forty years. These had

Britain counters Japan's interventions

27

not been used in the crises of 1884, 1894, 1898 or 1900. The Manchu Government was in dire financial straits. It could not fight the revolution. All this shows the extent to which Dr. Sun's trip to England had helped the Revolution of 1911.

Fruition

In this episode, we see the peace negotiations between the North and the South, the abdication of the Manchu Emperor, the resignation of Dr. Sun Yat-sen, and Yuan Shih-k'ai's assumption of authority.

Yuan Shih-k'ai

From 1909 to 1911, Yuan Shih-k'ai was in retirement at Chang-teh. In these two years, it was rumored time and again that he was about to re-emerge. During the P'ien Ma crisis in 1910, it was rumored that he was about to be called into service.[34] After the Huang-hua Kang incident, it was rumored that he was about to be appointed Viceroy of Kwangtung and Kwangsi (see American Minister to China Calhoun's telegram of September 5, 1911). After the outbreak at Wu-ch'ang, he received three major appointments within 30 days. On October 14, 1911 he was appointed Viceroy of the Hu-kwan provinces. On October 27, 1911 he was appointed Imperial Commissioner in charge of military affairs. On November 4, 1911 he was appointed Prime Minister in charge of military affairs. Yuan was at the height of his physical power (he was only 51). He had a clear knowledge of international affairs and of the domestic political situation. After he was called to power, he made two basic policy decisions in short order. These were: (1) to depend 30 per cent on military power and 70 per cent on political means to solve the issue, and (2) to negotiate through strength.

Yuan did not think much of the Revolutionary Army. Nevertheless, he appreciated the political difficulties. He thus secretly entrusted Liang Shih-i with political matters in the capital.[35] He was concentrating his attention not on the revolutionary South but on foreign diplomacy and members of the royal family.[36] Although he had no preference between constitutional monarchy and democratic republic, he created a new term "Chün-wei Kung-ho" (monarchical republic).[37] When Chang Ch'ien suggested that he should follow Washington's example, and when Yang Tu suggested that he should follow Napoleon's example, Yuan showed no opposition to either idea. However, he was dead set against playing the part of Tung Cho or Ts'ao Ts'ao, villains in Chinese history. He wanted to take over political power, but he was disinclined actually to put pressure on the Court. He wanted Empress Lung Yü to give up the throne, but he would not ask for it. He thought that only by acting in this way could he avoid the infamy of usurpation and become a hero of the transition. I do not think that this evaluation of Yuan's character is in any way unfair. At the time, Lo Ch'un-yung told Liang Ch'i-ch'ao that Yuan Shih-k'ai's mind was very difficult to fathom. Now that we have access to secret materials from various sources, we are in a better position to see his inner motives.

When Yuan was appointed Governor of

Yuan's political designs

Hupeh Province, he had no army under his direct command. He did not proceed to the front from Chang-teh until he was appointed Imperial Commissioner in charge of the various armies.[38] It was not until he was elected Prime Minister by the National Assembly by a vote of 87 to 78 that he was willing to accept the position.[39] He waited until the Manchu Court had abolished the system of "confidential memorials and direct-summons"[40] and announced the appointees to the posts of the Commander of the Imperial Guard and the Viceroyalty of the Hu and Kwang provinces before consenting to form a cabinet.[41] He waited until the artillery of the Imperial Guards had been sent to aid Shansi Province and the war materials had been sent to the Hupeh and Honan fronts before forcing Tsai Feng to resign as Prince Regent.[42] Having received the order from the Court to negotiate with the Revolutionary Army, he could no longer be condemned by the Royal Party for dealing with the enemy. Having received the order to organize a responsible cabinet, he could no longer be regarded by the National Assembly as attempting to isolate the Court by putting an end to the system of "confidential memorials and direct-summons." It was because of his superior knowledge and strategy, his calm maneuver and his unerring moves that he was able to emerge from this complicated struggle with the support of the North and the South.

In fact, Yuan's secret negotiations with the Revolutionary Army began before he was authorized to enter into them by the Court. When

Yuan's inner motives

he was the Viceroy of Hu-Kwang Province, he sent Liu Ch'eng-eng and Ts'ai T'ing-kan to negotiate with Li Yuan-hung. The first secret negotiation took place when Hankow was recovered on October 29, 1911. The second secret negotiation took place on the eve of Yuan's departure for the North (November 19, 1911). At that time, the situation at Wu-ch'ang and Hankow favored the revolutionaries. The preliminary contacts made no headway. Yuan knew that without a show of strength there could be no negotiation. He thus ordered Feng Kuo-chang to press his attack on Hanyang. As soon as Feng's army took Hanyang (November 27, 1911), he approached Sir John Jordan at Peking to have the British Consul at Hankow make an armistice proposal to both parties. Yuan's manipulation at this juncture was indeed very adroit.[43]

Secret negotiations

The peace negotiation between the North and the South was not initiated by Yuan alone. When Yuan was still at Chang-teh, Li Yuan-hung dispatched Chu Fei-huang, a Szechwanese, on a secret mission to see Yuan's son, Yuan K'e-ting, at Yuan Shang Ts'un. Chu's proposal contained three points: (1) dismissal of the Regent, Tsai-feng, (2) withdrawal of Feng Kuo-chang, and (3) support by the South for Yuan as President.[44] A written agreement was made between Yuan K'e-ting and Chu Fei-huang. On his way back to Hupeh, Chu had to pass through the front line held by Feng's men. Fearing that he might be searched, Chu tore up the agreement and swallowed the pieces! Ying Ch'ang, the Minister of War, was still in command at this time. No further proposal was thus made on Yuan's part. However, by the time Hanyang was taken and a peace proposal made by the British Consul, Tsai Feng had resigned and Feng Kuo-chang was on the point of being transferred. Thus, of the three points agreed to at Yuan Shang Ts'un, only the last point — support for Yuan as President — remained to be fulfilled. Li Yuan-hung was thus obliged to submit his peace proposal to the various provinces.

Tsai Feng relinquished his regency on November 6, 1911. Empowered by the Court to deal with the general situation, Yuan sent T'ang Shao-yi, Yang Shih-ch'i, and Yen Hsiu on November 8 as delegates to negotiate a peace with the revolutionaries in Hankow. The negotiation took place in Shanghai between the Northern delegates and Wu T'ing-fang, who represented the South. Soon after the talk began, Yuan's subordinates approached Huang Hsing's men in a new endeavor to reach a secret agreement.

Open negotiations for peace

Thus, the peace negotiations between the North and the South in 1911 took place on two levels. The official peace conference took place in the Municipal Hall between T'ang Shao-yi, who represented the North, and Wu T'ing-fang, who represented the South. The secret conference took place in the Wen Ming Bookstore on Yunnan Road in Shanghai. In this conference, Liao Yü-ch'un of the Pao-ting Cadets Training School, represented the North and Ku Chung-shen, Chief of Staff of the Kiangsu-Chekiang Army Headquarters, represented the South.[45] Liao Yü-ch'un was Chin Yun-p'eng's (Chief Advisor to Tuan Ch'i-jui, the Commander of the Northern Army at the time) private representative. Ku Chung-shen was Huang Hsing's private representative. The official peace conference started on December 18, 1911 and was interrupted on January 12, 1912. The secret peace conference started on December 19, 1911 and the agreement was signed on the next day.

The secret agreement which was signed contained five articles:

1. Establishment of a republican form of government.

The secret agreement

2. Favorable treatment to be extended to the Emperor and the royal family.

3. The person who first overthrew the Manchu Dynasty was to become President.

4. The combatants on both sides were to be absolved from all responsibility for hostile acts.

5. A provisional parliament was to be convened to restore peace and order.

When Dr. Sun Yat-sen assumed the presidency on January 1, 1912, the following five points were contained in his final proposal:

1. The abdication of the Manchu Emperor. The Yuan cabinet was to notify the ministers of the foreign powers in China of the abdication, and the diplomatic corps was to notify the Nanking Government.

2. A republican form of government to be declared by Yuan Shih-k'ai.

3. Dr. Sun Yat-sen to resign before the

Senate upon receipt of the notification from the diplomatic corps.

4. Yuan Shih-k'ai to be elected President by the Senate.

5. Yuan Shih-k'ai to swear that he would abide by the Constitution drawn up by the Senate before taking over authority.

Comparing the terms of the secret agreement between Liao and Ku with the terms of Sun's demand, we can see that the former agreement was the forerunner of the latter. The emphasis of the former was on substantial matters, while that of the latter was on procedure. The former was aimed at overthrowing the Manchu Dynasty, while the latter was directed at instituting precautionary measures against Yuan. We can also see that although the abdication edict was not issued until February 12, 1912, the Empire was already lost to the Manchus by December 20, 1911.

Sun's real intention

The day Liao and Ku reached an agreement, December 20, 1911, Dr. Sun Yat-sen was still on his way back to China. However, from his conversations with Hu Han-min and Chu Chih-hsing in Hongkong[46] we see that he agreed with the idea of supporting Yuan as the President. We have no direct evidence as to whether Yuan approved of the secret agreement. However, from the fact that Liao Yü-ch'un was decorated in the first year of the Republic, Yuan's attitude was quite apparent.[47]

It may seem strange that the formal negotiation should have broken down following the conclusion of the secret agreement. This came about because of Dr. Sun Yat-sen's election to the Presidency. The agreement provided for the person who first overthrew the Manchu regime to become the President. Sun arrived in Shanghai on December 25, 1911 and was elected on December 29. On January 1, 1912, he went to Nanking to assume the post. At that time, the Manchu regime had yet to be overthrown. Yuan's side naturally considered that to be a violation of the terms of the agreement. Sun also seemed to have taken this into consideration. Thus, he wired Yuan the day before and the day after his assumption of office (December 31, 1911 and January 2, 1912) assuring him that he was taking the post only temporarily and that he would vacate it in his favor. Nevertheless, Yuan accepted T'ang Shao-i's resignation on January 2, 1912 and broke off the formal talks.

This setback could now be overcome only through an intermediary who was unusually persuasive. At this juncture, Wang Ching-wei appeared on the scene and was ready to play a decisive role. In 1911, Wang was serving a life sentence for plotting to assassinate Tsai Feng on March 28, 1910 in Peking. In the latter part of November in 1911, Chang Ming-ch'i, Viceroy of the Kwang provinces, memorialized the throne, asking for his release.[48] According to the imperial decree that released him, Wang was supposed to be handed over to Chang Ming-ch'i and leave Peking immediately. However, Yuan having just taken over the post of the Prime-Ministership, secretly instructed Yang Tu to keep Wang in Peking. When Yuan arrived in Peking he had several conversations

Wang Ching-wei's secret mission

with Wang late at night. On the eve of Wang's departure for the South, December 26, 1911, Yuan entertained him and asked his son, Yuan K'e-ting, to become his sworn brother. When T'ang Shao-i and Yang Shih-ch'i went to Hankow for the peace talks, Wang accompanied them on the train as far as Ch'ang Hsin-tien. The relation between Yuan and Wang was indeed very close.

Sun Yat-sen arrived in Shanghai on December 25, 1911. Wang Ching-wei left Peking on December 27. Although he was nominally to serve as Wu T'ing-fang's advisor, he was in fact Yuan Shih-k'ai's secret envoy. At that time, Liang Shih-i, who was in Peking, knew what Yuan had in mind better than anybody else. Before Wang Ching-wei left Peking, Liang had drafted a three-step program to force the Manchu Court to abdicate. The first step was for the Chinese ministers abroad to make a joint request for abdication. The second was for the cabinet members (not including the Prime Minister) to make a public request for a decision. The third was for the commanders at the front to offer a joint threat.[49] Just when the first step was taken (the telegram from the ministers abroad headed by Lu Cheng-hsiang[50] requesting abdication was received on January 3, 1912), Sun Yat-sen had been elected President in Nanking. The North did not know of Sun's real intention, while the South was ignorant of the Northern program. It was at this moment that Wang Ching-wei arrived. He could not have arrived at a more opportune and propitious moment.

Less than two weeks after Wang's arrival in Shanghai, the peace talks were revived. On January 13, 1912, Liang Shih-i wired Wu Ting-fang informing him that arrangements had been made for the Manchu abdication and asking him what assurance the South would give to support Yuan. As soon as Dr. Sun learned about the wire, he replied on January 15, 1912 assuring the North that he would resign from the Presidency as soon as the Manchus abdicated and Yuan declared his intention to support the Republic.[51]

At this point, an incident occurred which was expected at first to upset the peace conference. On the very day that Sun Yat-sen replied to Wu T'ing fang's inquiry, an attempt was made by Chang Hsien-p'ei and Huang Chih-meng to assassinate Yuan outside the Tung-hua Gate at Peking. As the South was suspected of being behind the plot, it served to clear Yuan of whatever suspicion the Manchus entertained. This served to speed up the peace conference rather than to upset it. On January 19, 1912, the cabinet members Hu Wei-te, Chao Ping-chun, and Liang Shih-i submitted a joint memorial stating that the monarchical system could no longer be maintained and requesting Empress Lung Yü to make a decision. On January 21, 1912, an imperial conference was called to discuss the abdication. On January 26, 1912, forty-seven commanders at the front, led by Tuan Ch'i-jui, sent a joint telegram supporting republicanism. All three steps proposed by Liang Shih-i had now been taken. By this time, Sun Yat-sen's final five-point demand had arrived

Arrangements for the Manchu abdication

in Peking (January 22, 1912). The Empress issued a decree making Yuan Shih-k'ai a marquis of the first order on January 23, 1912. Yuan had now received promises from both the North and the South. In such a predicament, he declined, on the one hand, the marquisate and made a gesture, on the other hand, of declining the presidency.[52]

The peace conference between the North and the South was still proceeding on two other levels at this time. The open conference was conducted by telegram between Yuan and Wu T'ing-fang. The secret conference was conducted by cable through Liang Shih-i and T'ang Shao-i. In the open conference both sides resorted to official talk, high-sounding phrases and even mutual recrimination. In the secret conference, each side appealed to the other for an understanding of its difficulties. Attempts were made to reach a compromise. From Wu T'ing-fang's records, we see that the abdication could have taken place on January 21, 1912. It was delayed because the Nanking cabinet insisted that Dr. Sun Yat-sen should resign only after the Powers had recognized the Chinese Republic. During this delay, the Imperial Clan Party started its activities. P'u Wei and Shan Ch'i went secretly to Fengtien in Manchuria. Talk of Japanese intervention on behalf of the Manchus became more open. At the same time, the Banner troops of the Imperial Guards were also unstable. At one time, Yuan's aides planned to move the government to Tientsin for safety. In the South, there was some misunderstanding between Wu T'ing-

Politics delay abdication

fang and Sun Yat-sen. It was not until Ts'ao K'un (Yuan's subordinate) had led his Third Division back to Peking from Niang Tzu Kuan that the Imperial Guards backed down. When the second Imperial Conference was called, Tsai Feng and I K'uang did not appear. Empress Lung Yü thus decided to abdicate (January 30, 1912). Now Yuan and the Northern commanders began to bargain seriously over the terms of favorable treatment for the royal family. The three characters "Jan Huang Ti" ("The Abdicated Emperor") were finally eliminated. Having obtained the right to reside in the Imperial Palace and further rights concerning the organization and payment of the Imperial Guards, the Court issued an edict of three hundred and fourteen characters on February 12, 1912, which put an end to two hundred and sixty-seven years of imperial rule.[53]

The abdication edit was drafted by Chang Ch'ien in Shanghai with the approval of the South. (This was also mentioned in Hu Han-min's letter to Chang Hsiao-jo.) The edict contained the clause empowering Yuan Shih-k'ai to organize a republican government. As the clause was not in the original draft, the version was of course unpalatable to the South. The South, on its part, unilaterally changed the presidential form of government to the cabinet form following Sun Yat-sen's resignation. This countered, in a way, the Northern move. The abdication edict was issued on February 12, 1912. Yuan's message in support of republicanism reached Nanking on February 13.[54] Sun Yat-sen thereupon resigned the presidency on

The abdication edict

the same day. The Senate elected Yuan President by the unanimous vote of 37 to 0 on February 14th.[55]

This drama, with its military and civil elements, was superbly played by an outstanding cast. Even now, we must admit that the outcome was the best one possible for the time. If it had been otherwise, hostilities would have broken out again between the North and the South, Japan might have intervened militarily, and the situation which took place in Manchuria following the Mukden incident of 1931 might have taken place at this time. Yuan's later attempt to establish a monarchy was, of course, a violation of the terms of the agreement which he had so solemnly sworn to uphold. Nevertheless, in 1911 both sides were willing to compromise in order to avoid bloodshed and to prevent foreign intervention. They finally brought about the creation of a unified Republic of China.

NOTES

[1] Karl R. Kopper, *The Open Society and Its Enemies*, p. 361.

[2] *Journal of the History of Ideas*, Vol. 16, No. 3, June 3, 1955, p. 421.

[3] *Kuo-fu Nien-p'u* ("Sun Yat-sen's Chronology"), Vol. 1, p. 56 and 134.

[4] *Ibid.*, p. 152.

[5] *Hsin-hai Ko-ming* ("The Revolution of 1911"). Published by the Chinese Historical Society, Vol. 1, p. 253. References in *The Uprising of Hung Ch'üan-fu* in the Palace Archives and Feng Tzu-yu's *Hua Hsing Hui and Kuang Fu Hui*.

[6] Chang Huang-hsi, *T'ao Ch'eng-chang Ko-ming Shih* ("The Revolution of T'ao Ch'eng-chang"). In 1908, T'ao Ch'eng-chang attempted to oust Sun Yat-sen and have Huang Hsing made Tsung-li of the T'ung Meng Hui. His attempt failed.

[7] In April, 1901, the Cheng Wu Ch'ü (Political Bureau) was established; in May, 1902, the Fa Lu Kuan (Law Institute); in May, 1903, the Ts'ai Cheng Chü (Finance Bureau); in August, 1903, the Shang Pu (Ministry of Commerce); in December, 1903, the Lien Ping Chü (Army Training Bureau); and in October, 1904, the Hsueh Pu (Ministry of Education). The Reform movement was in full swing.

[8] Holcombe, Arthur N., *The Chinese Revolution* (1930); Woodhead H. G. W., *The Truth About the Chinese Republic* (1925).

[9] Hu Ssu-Ching, *Kuo Wen Pei Ch-eng.*

[10] Wei Yuan-k'uang, *Chien Ping Chih.*

[11] *Liang Jen Kung Nien-p'u Chang P'ien* ("Liang Ch'i Chao's Chronology"), Vol. 2, p. 318.

[12] Wei Yuan-k'uang wrote in his book, *Kuang-Hsuan Ch'ien Tsai:* "When I-K'uang was in charge of the government, he neglected political affairs and was interested only in taking bribes. Each political appointment had a price. Once an aspirant to the post of minister to England approached him with a bribe. Having offered the bribe, he thought that the matter was settled. The next day,

he found himself appointed to Italy rather than to England, for the amount he offered was inadequate."

[13] In settling the problem of private shares in the Szechwan-Hankow and Canton-Hankow Railroads, Hunan, Hupei, and Kwantung provinces promised to redeem them in cash. Only Szechwan was reluctant. *See* Wang Jen-wen, *Ssu-ch'uan Lu Shih Tsui Yen;* Chou Shan-p'ei, *Hsin-hai Ssu-Ch'uan Shih-pien Chih Wo;* and the *Case of the Szechuan Railroad* in the Palace Archives.

[14] Chang Hsing-yen's own account in *Su Pao An Shih Mo Chi* ("An Account of the Su Pao Case") ; Wu Chih-hui, *Shang Hai Su Pao Chi Shih* ("An Account of the Case of the Shanghai Su Pao").

[15] Tang Liang-li, *The Inner History of the Chinese Revolution* (1950).

[16] In September, 1907, a decree was issued to establish Tzu Cheng Yuan (National Assembly), and in November, the provinces were ordered to convene the Tzu I Chu (provincial assemblies). *See* Ts'ang Fu, "I-hui Chi Cheng-tang" ("Parliament and the Political Party") in the *Hsin-hai Ko-ming* ("Revolution of 1911"), Vol. 4, p. 67.

[17] Details in Cameron, *The Reform Movement in China, 1898-1912.*

[18] Wu Lu-cheng took part in Tang Ts'ai-ch'ang's revolutionary activities at Ta-t'ung. This brought him into contact with Liang Ch'i-ch'ao. When Chang Shao-tseng and other military leaders at Luan-chou made demands on the government with military backing, Wu was ordered by the government to deal with the matter. Instead of carrying out government orders, he planned secretly with Chang Shao-tseng and Lan T'ien-wei to lead their troops to the north. On November 6, 1911, Liang Ch'i-ch'ao returned secretly via Dairen hoping to see Wu. On the day of his arrival in Dairen, Wu was assassinated. He then went to Feng-t'ien hoping to join Lan T'ien-wei. Lan had, however, left for Peking. The garrison at Feng-t'ien tried to harm Liang. Hsiung Ping-san informed him and urged him to leave. He then went to Dairen and returned to Japan. *Liang Jen Kung Nien P'u Ch'ang P'ien,* Vol. 2, p. 343.

[19] Homer Lea was a talented military strategist. (He was mistaken to be an American military officer in the *Kuo-fu Nien-p'u,* Vol. 1, p. 296.) As he failed to qualify for the Army owing to his physical disabilities, he devoted himself to the study of military strategy. He wrote the following books: *The Valor of Ignorance* (1908), *Vermillion Pencil* (1908), and the *Day of Saxon.* Some of his prophecies, such as that Japan would take the Philippines and that England would decline, have come true. However, few Americans knew of his works. When war broke out with Japan in the Philippines in 1941, a Philippine student was found to have in his possession a map showing in detail the strategic areas of the islands. These happened to agree in many cases with the plan that General MacArthur had drawn up. MacArthur's headquarters thought at first that the student was a spy. Upon inquiry, it was found that the map had come from a book written by Homer Lea thirty-three years ago. This established his fame, and his book was reprinted. The above incident was related in a book on Homer Lea by Clare Boothe. Lea was a good friend of Dr. Sun Yat-sen. He offered his services to Sun as a military advisor. When Dr. Sun assumed the Presidency in Nanking on January 1, 1912, Lea was the only foreign guest to take part in the ceremony. On that occasion, he warned Dr. Sun of the danger of Japan as an enemy to both China and the United States. In less than three months, he returned to America on account of illness and died in November of that year in San Francisco.

[20] State Department, *Foreign Relations.*

[21] *Foreign Relations,* 1910-1912.

[22] *See* Huang Hsing's speech on "The Causes and Results of the April 27th Revolution in Canton."

[23] Wu Hsing-han, *Wu-ch'ang Ch'i-i San Jih Chi* ("A Three Day Account of the Wu-chang Uprising").

[24] Ts'ao Ya-po, "Wuchang Uprising" in *Hsin-hai Ko-ming* ("Revolution of 1911"), compiled by the Chinese Historical Society, Vol. V, p. 104.

[25] U.S. Minister to Japan Schuyler's telegram No. 566 in *Foreign Relations,* 1910-12.

[26] Jordan to Foreign Secretary Grey, telegram 8p/342.

[27] Hu Ying's seven-point note was sent to the consular body in Hankow on October 11, 1911. The full text and the declaration of neutrality by the foreign consuls in Hankow are in *Hsin-hai Ko-ming,* Vol. 5.

[28] According to Chang I-po's account of the Navy's part in the Revolution, Ho Wei-sheng, the chief wireless operator on the cruiser Hai Ch'ou, Chin Chuan-chang, the chief wireless opera-on the cruiser Hai Yung, and Chang I-po, the chief wireless operator on the cruiser Hai Shen, had exchanged secret English codes with the revolutionaries and they agreed not to aim their fire at the revolutionary forces. Only four or five people knew of this episode.

[29] Sun Yat-sen, *Ko-ming Yüan-ch'i* ("The Causes of the Revolution") .

[30] On October 15, 1911, the Japanese Government cabled U.S. Secretary of State Knox to the effect that although the Chinese Government had requested Japan to send troops to put down the revolution, Japan would not take action until her interests were seriously menaced and until the powers had requested her to intervene. However, the cable added that should the revolution spread to Manchuria, Japan would send troops without consulting the powers and that 20,000 troops were expected to reach Peking.

On December 2, 1911, Foreign Minister Uchida Yasuya informed the American Ambassador Bryan that if hostilities between the North and the South should continue, the Japanese Government would find it necessary to consider intervention.

On December 18, 1911, the Japanese Chargé d'Affaire in Washington proposed in a note to the State Department the establishment of a nominal Manchu regime under the joint guarantee of the powers. (The U.S. and Germany turned down the proposal. England was also opposed to the idea.)

[31] *See* U.S. Minister to Japan Schuyler's telegram to the State Department.

[32] After Dr. Sun had assumed the Presidency, the Japanese Government indicated, on the one hand, that it wanted to support the Manchu Government, while on the other hand, it sent Matsui to China to consult with the Nanking Government on joint action against Yuan Shih-kai. *See* the conversation between Dr. Sun and Charles D. Kennedy, the American Counselor, in Nanking in January, 1912, in *Foreign Relations,* 1910-1912, p. 67.

[33] *British Parliamentary Report*, P8/374.

[34] *London Times,* December 17, 1917.

[35] *San-shui Hsien-sheng Nien-p'u,* Vol. 1, p. 100.

[36] Shang Ping-ho, *Hsin-jen Ch'un Ch'iu.*

[37] Conversation between Lo Ch'un-yung and Yuan Shih-kai in *Liang Jen-kung Nien-p'u Ch'ang-p'ien,* Vol. 2, p. 350.

[38] The *London Times* of October 14, 1911 carried a report of Yuan's six demands as follows: (1) Convening of parliament; (2) Responsible cabinet; (3) Amnesty for party members; (4) Comforting the New Army; (5) United military command; and (6) Full financial support.

[39] Yuan Shih-k'ai was appointed premier on November 4. The appointment was approved by the Tzu Cheng Yuan on November 8.

[40] This is a system whereby the memorials may be presented to the throne directly by the officials and the officials may be summoned without going through the Premier.

[41] Shang Ping-ho, *Hsin-Jen Ch'un-ch'iu.*

[42] Lo Ch'un-yung's letter to Liang Ch'i-ch'ao on December 13, 1911.

[43] Confidential telegram No. 366 from Jordan to Grey and confidential telegram No. 351 from Jordan to the British Consul in Hankow.

[44] Shang Ping-ho, *loc. cit.*

[45] Ch'ien Chi-po, *Hsin-hai I-ho Pieh-chi* ("An Account of the Peace Negotiations in 1911").

[46] *Kuo-fu Nien-p'u,* Vol. 1, p. 286.

[47] Liao Shao-yu, *Hsin Chung-kuo Wu-chuang Ho-p'ing Chieh-chueh Chi* ("An Account of the Peaceful Solution of New China's Armed Forces").

[48] Chang Huang-hsi, *Wang Chao-ming Keng-hsü Pei-tai Kung-tz'u* ("Wang Chao-ming's Testimony Following His Arrest in 1910").

[49] *Liang Yen-sun Nien-p'u* ("Liang Yen-sun's Chronology"), p. 105-106.

[50] Lu Cheng-hsiang, later known as Dom Pierre-Célestin Lou Tseng-tsiang, became a monk at the abbey of Saint-André near Bruges in Belgium. He was made the titular abbot of St. Peters of Ghent in 1946 and died on January 15, 1949.

[51] Wu T'ing-fang, *Kuang-tu-lu Kung-ho Kuang-chien Lu.*

[52] *Kuan-tu lu Kung-ho Kuan-chien Lu* contains Liang Shih-i's telegram to Wu Ting-fang in which Liang said: "Yuan had no intention of becoming President. It was because of foreign and domestic pressure that he agreed to assume the post temporarily so as to save the situation. Now that the situation is so difficult [his assumption of the post] may give rise to complications without in any way helping the situation. It is better for Mr. Sun to continue. . . ."

[53] Empress Lung Yü's abdication decree reads as follows: "Owing to the uprising of the Min Chün (People's Army) and the response of the various provinces which brought unrest to the whole country and caused suffering among the people, Yuan Shih-k'ai was authorized to send delegates to discuss the general situation with Min Chün representatives. The object was to convene a National Assembly and decide upon the form of the state publicly. It has been two months now and no suitable measure has been adopted. The North and the South still stand facing each other. Business and other pursuits have come to a standstill. As long as the form of the state is not settled, the people will not enjoy peace. The people of the whole country are now in favor of a republican form of government. This form is advocated by the Southern provinces and supported by the Northern generals. *The Mandate of Heaven is manifested through the wish of the people.* I would not want to

go against their wish just to uphold the honor of one family. Thus, in view of the general situation and public opinion, the Emperor and I have decided to let the whole people share in the power of government and to establish a republican constitutional state. This will, on the one hand, satisfy the yearning of the people for peace, and on the other, comply with the idea of the ancient sages that the Empire belongs to the public. Tzu Cheng Yuan has elected Yuan Shih-k'ai to be the Premier. During this transitional period, a way must be found to unite the North and the South. We now entrust Yuan with full power to organize a republican form of government and negotiate with the Min Chün for national unity. It is hoped that the people will live in peace and that the five races — Manchus, Chinese, Mongols, Mohammedans, and Tibetans — will continue to unite in preserving their territories and forming a Chung-hua Min-kuo (Republic of China). The Emperor and I will then withdraw and enjoy the honor that the people accord us. We shall witness the successful establishment of good government. Is this not an excellent prospect?"

[54] In a telegram supporting the republican form, Yuan Shih-k'ai said: "That the republican form is the best form of government is generally recognized by the world. That we are able to change from monarchy to this form in one leap is the result of many years' effort on your part. It is at the same time the great fortune of the country. The Ta Ch'ing Emperor has issued a decree abdicating the throne and I have counter-signed it. The day the decree is promulgated marks the end of the monarchy and the beginning of the republic. From now on, we shall strive to make it a success and prevent the monarchical form from ever being reintroduced in China. . . ."

[55] Lin Chang-min, *Ts'an-I-yuan I-nien Shih* ("One Year's History of the Senate").

Glossary
of Chinese Names

Anking	安慶
Chang Chi	張繼
Chang Ch'ien	張謇
Chang Feng-hui	張鳳翽
Chang Hsiao-jo	張孝若
Chang Hsien-p'ei	張先培
Chang Hsing-yen	章行嚴
Chang Hsun	張勳
Chang Huang-hsi	張篁谿
Chang I-po	張懌伯
Chang Ming-ch'i	張鳴岐
Chang P'ei-chueh	張培爵
Changsha	長沙
Chang Shao-tseng	張紹曾
Chang Shih-ch'ao	章士釗
Chang T'ai-yen	章太炎
Ch'ang Jung-ch'ing	常榮清
Ch'ang Hsin-tien	長辛店
Ch'ao-chou	潮州
Chao Ch'un-ch'eng	趙純誠
Chao Ping-chun	趙秉鈞
Chao Sheng	趙聲
Chen Ch'i-mei	陳其美
Chen-kiang Tu-tu	鎮江都督

Chen-nan-kuan

Chen Tien-hua

Cheng Kuei-Kuang

Cheng Shih-liang

Cheng Wu Ch'ü

Ch'eng Te-ch'uan

Ch'i Nu Hu

Ch'i Yao-san

Chiang I-wu

Chiang-wu Tang

Chiao Ta-feng

Chien Chi-po

Ch'ien Ting

Chien Ping Chih

Chih-chiang

Chin Chuan-chang

Ch'ing-lien

Ch'ing Shan

Ching Shih Chung

Ch'iu Ching

Chou Shan-p'ei

Chü Cheng

Chu Chia-pao

Chu Chih-hsiang

Chu Ching-lan

關華光良處全湖珊武堂峯博鼎志江章廉山鐘瑾培正寶信瀾

南天奎士務德女權翊武達基錢冰墊豫欽青世秋善居家執慶

鎮陳程鄭政程七齊蔣講焦錢　堅　金　警　周　朱朱朱

Chu Fei-huang	朱芾煌
Chün-Cheng-fen-fu Tu-tu	軍政分府都督
Chün-cheng-fu Tu-tu	軍政府都督
"Chun-wei Kung-ho"	君位共和
Chung-hua Min-kuo Chün-cheng-fu Kiang-su Tu-tu-fu	中華民國軍政府江蘇都督府
Chungking	重慶
Constitutional Society, The	憲政會
Empress Dowager Tz'u-hsi	慈禧
Empress Lung Yü	隆裕
Fa Lu Kuan	法律館
Fan Yuan-lien	范源濂
Fang Ch'eng	防城
Feng Kuo-chang	馮國璋
Feng Tzu-yu	馮自由
Fu-han-chun Ta-t'ung-ling	復漢軍大統領
Fu yu Piao	富有票
Hai Ch'ou	海籌
Hai Shen	海琛
Hai Yung	海容
Heng-chi-kang	橫枝崗
Ho-k'ou	河口
Ho Wei-sheng	何渭生
Hsia Chih-shih	夏之時
Hsien-feng	咸豐

Hsin Chung-kuo Wu-chang Ho-p'ing Chieh-chueh Chi	新中國武裝和平解決記
Hsin-hai I-ho Pieh-chi	辛亥議和別記
Hsin-hai Ko-ming	辛亥革命
Hsin-hai Ssu-Ch'uan Shih-pien Chih Wo	辛亥四川事變之我
Hsin-jen Ch'un Ch'iu	辛壬春秋
Hsin-min Ts'ung-pao	新民叢報
Hsing Chung Hui	興中會
Hsiung Ch'eng-chi	熊成基
Hsiung Ping-K'un	熊秉坤
Hsu Hsi-ling	徐錫麟
Hsu Hsueh-ch'iu	許雪秋
Hsu Shao-cheng	徐紹楨
Hsueh Pu	學部
Hu Chün-cheng-fu Tu-tu	滬軍政府都督
Hu Han-min	胡漢民
Hu Ssu-ching	胡思敬
Hu Wei-te	胡惟德
Hu Ying	胡瑛
Hua Hsing Hui	華興會
Hua Hsing Hui and Kuang Fu Hui	華興會及光復會
Huang Chih-meng	黃之萌
Huang-hua-Kang	黃花崗
Huang Kang	黃岡
Huang K'e-ch'iang	黃克強
Huang Ming-t'ang	黃明堂

52

Hui-chou	惠州
Hung Chuan-fu	洪全福
"I-hui Chi Cheng-tang"	議會及政黨
I K'uang	奕劻
"Jan Huang Ti"	讓皇帝
Jung-hsien	榮縣
Jung Lu	榮祿
K'ang Yu-wei	康有為
Kao Lao Hui	哥老會
Ko-ming Yüan-ch'i	革命緣起
Ku Chung-shen	顧忠琛
Kuang Fu Hui	光復會
Kuang-hsü	光緒
Kuang Hsuan Ch'ien Tsai	光宣僉載
Kuang-tu-lu Kung-ho Kuang-chien Lu	觀渡廬共和關鍵錄
Kung Chin Hui	共進會
Kung Ho	共和
Kuo-fu Nien-p'u	國父年譜
Kuo-min Kung-pao	國民公報
Kuo Wen Pei Ch'eng	國聞備乘
Lan T'ien-wei	藍天蔚
Li Chi-t'ang	李紀堂
Li-ling	醴陵
Li P'ing-shu	李平書
Li Yuan-hung	黎元洪

Liang Ch'i-ch'ao		梁 啟 超
Liang-Hu		兩 湖
Liang Jen Kung Nien-p'u Chang P'ien	梁任公年譜長編	
Liang-Kwang		兩 廣
Liang Mu-hsing		梁 慕 信
Liang Shih-i		梁 士 詒
Liao Shao-yu		廖 少 游
Liao Yü-ch'un		廖 宇 春
Lien Ping Chü		練 兵 處
Lin Chang-min		林 長 民
Lin Kuei		林 奎
Lin-shih Cheng-fu	臨 時	林 政 府
Lin Shu-ch'eng		林 述 慶
Literary Society, The		文 學 社
Liu Ch'eng-eng		劉 承 恩
Liu Hsun		劉 詢
Liu K'uei-i	劉	揆 一
Liu Tao-i	劉	道 一
Liu-yang		瀏 陽
Liu Yao-ch'eng	劉	垚 澂
Lo Ch'un-yung	羅	惇 融
Lo P'ei-chin	羅	佩 金
Lu Cheng-hsiang	陸	徵 祥
Lu Hao-tung	陸	皓 東
Lu Jung-t'ing	陸	榮 廷

54

Shang Pu	商部
Shen Chin	沈藎
Sheng Hsuan-huai	盛宣懷
Shih Chien-ju	史堅如
Shih Wang Ta Shan	十萬大山
Shou-chou	壽州
Shu-chun Cheng-fu	蜀軍政府
Shu-pei Tu-tu	蜀北都督
Ssu-ch'uan Lu Shih Tsui Yen	四川路事罪言
Ssu-ch'uang Tu-tu	四川都督
Su Pao	蘇報
Su Pao An Shih Mo Chi	蘇報案始末記
Sun Tao-jen	孫道仁
Sun Wu	孫武
Sun Yat-sen	孫逸仙
Sung Chiao-jen	宋教仁
Ta-han Chün-cheng-fu	大漢軍政府
"Ta Ming Shun T'ien Kuo"	大明順天國
Ta-t'ung	大通
T'an Jen-feng	譚人鳳
T'an Yen-k'ai	譚延闓
T'ang Chi-yao	唐繼堯
T'ang Hua-lung	湯化龍
T'ang Shao-yi	唐紹儀
T'ang Shou-ch'ien	湯壽潛

T'ang Ts'ai-ch'ang	唐才常
T'ao Ch'eng-chang	陶成章
T'ao Ch'i-sheng	陶啟勝
Teng Tzu-yu	鄧子瑜
Tsai-feng	載灃
Tsai Hsün	載洵
Tsai T'ao	載濤
Tsai Tse	載澤
Ts'ai Cheng Chü	財政處
Ts'ai O	蔡鍔
Ts'ai Ting-kan	蔡廷幹
Ts'ai Yuan-p'ei	蔡元培
Ts'an I-yuan I-nien Shih	參議院一年史
Ts'ao K'un	曹錕
Ts'ao Ts'ao	曹操
Ts'ao Ya-po	曹亞伯
Tseng Sheng-chai	曾省齋
Tsou Jung	鄒容
Tsung-ssu-ling	總司令
Tu Ch'ien	杜潛
Tu-tu	都督
Tuan Ch'i-jui	段祺瑞
Tung Cho	董卓
T'ung-chih	同治
T'ung-chih Chun	同志軍

58

Yen Hsiu		修
Ying Ch'ang		昌
Yu Chih-mo		謨
Yu Ch'ing Li		里
Yuan K'e-ting		定 村 凱
Yuan Shang Ts'un	嚴 廕 之 慶 克 上 世
Yuan Shih-k'ai	禹 餘 袁 洹 袁

修謨里定村凱
嚴廕之慶克上世
禹餘袁洹袁